JAPAN INC.

JAPAN INC.

An Introduction to
Japanese Economics
(The Comic Book)

Shōtarō Ishinomori

Translated by Betsey Scheiner
With an introduction by Peter Duus

UNIVERSITY OF CALIFORNIA PRESS

Berkeley   Los Angeles

The persons and organizations appearing in this book are fictitious
and have no relation to actual persons or organizations.

University of California Press
Berkeley and Los Angeles, California

University of California Press, Ltd.
London, England

© 1988 by
The Regents of the University of California

© 1986 by Shōtarō Ishinomori
Published in Japan by Nihon Keizai Shimbun, Inc.
Reprinted by permission of Nihon Keizai Shimbun, Inc.

Library of Congress Cataloging-in-Publication Data

Ishinomori, Shōtarō, 1938–
   Japan Inc.

   1. Japan—Economic conditions—1945–   —Caricatures
and cartoons.   2. Japan—Economic policy—1945–   —
Caricatures and cartoons.   3. Japan—Foreign economic
relations—United States—Caricatures and cartoons.
4. United States—Foreign economic relations—Japan—
Caricatures and cartoons.   I. Title.
HC462.9.I74   1988   330.952′048′0207   87-36766
ISBN 0-520-06288-4 (alk. paper)
ISBN 0-520-06289-2 (pbk. : alk. paper)

Printed in the United States of America

Contents

A Note to the American Edition

The preparation of *Japan Inc.* for English-speaking readers raised several technical problems, because Japanese comics read from right to left, Western comics from left to right. One solution was to offer readers a brief encounter with Japanese culture by printing the book in its original order, with a warning that they should begin reading at what they would usually consider the end. This method seemed a little too complicated, however, to impose on a comic book. Another solution was simply to flip the pages and print them backward, but this one failed to take into account the number of panels in which the artwork and writing—Japanese, English, or Arabic—were combined. If these pages were flipped, a mirror would have been needed to make them legible. In the end, we opted for a selective flipping: panels were reversed if necessary to clarify the flow of the dialogue; otherwise, they were printed as they appear in the Japanese edition. As a result, some of the characters may suddenly appear to develop left-handed tendencies.

Like any respectable comic book, this one was filled with the Japanese equivalents for words like BAM! CRASH! and BOING!—words that seem obvious in context but are often difficult to translate. What, for example, is the English for *koro koro,* the sound a pencil makes rolling across a table? In general, such words have been left untranslated. Since their function is partially decorative, they can be considered part of the artwork, or enterprising readers can devise their own translations.

In Japan, it is customary to write Japanese names with the family name first but to leave Western names in Western order. Thus, the creator of this comic book is known in Japan as Ishinomori Shōtarō; the author of *Wealth of Nations* is known as Adam Smith. This convention is followed throughout the Introduction and pages of *Japan Inc.*

Introduction

It may come as a surprise that Japanese high school students are among the most avid readers of comic books and magazines in the world. How could such exemplary high-achieving young people, whose remarkable performance on math and science tests has been touted as one of the keys to Japan's economic success, be addicted to reading comics? Yet the facts are clear. A 1987 survey by the Japanese Youth Research Institute discovered that even though only 15 percent of American senior high school students read comics, 69 percent of their Japanese counterparts do. Does this mean that American precollegiate education is not in such bad shape after all? And does it portend a turnaround in the economic future of both countries?

The answer is: probably not. These statistics merely reflect how deeply comic strips, comic books, and comic magazines have become rooted in Japanese popular culture. To think of Japanese comics simply as entertainment for lowbrows is to miss the mark. In Japan the comics, like television, have become a powerful medium for entertainment, for the transmission of knowledge, and for the diffusion of values. Indeed, the term "comics" is a misnomer. Most *manga* (the generic term for cartoons, narrative strips, and animated films) are not at all funny. The most ambitious strive to achieve artistic and intellectual respectability. Nor is the readership of comic publications limited to the adolescent or the preadolescent. It is not at all uncommon to find the coffee shops near elite national universities well stocked with comics for their student customers or to see a blue-suited young white-collar worker flipping through a weekly comic magazine as thick as a telephone book on his way home from work.

Until recently, the U.S. comic book industry had fallen on hard times. Americans of a certain age will remember reading comic books of two types—the good, clean, wholesome kind that your mother liked, and the bad, horrific revolting kind that you had to sneak into the house. The collapse of the American comic book industry came in the 1950s when the bad kind seemed to be crowding out the good. The mothers of America, together with their allies in Congress, the churches, and the schools, succeeded in forcing the comic book industry to adopt the Comic Book Authority, a self-censorship system not unlike the old Hayes office in Hollywood. The result was the withering away of the industry during the next two decades. Even today, when there is a revival of comic book publishing, variety and output remain limited compared to Japan's.

In Japan, however, the production of comic books and magazines represents a major activity of the Japanese publishing industry. There are comic books and magazines catering to nearly every conceivable taste, from the trashy to the edifying. In 1980 comic books and magazines accounted for more than a quarter of all books and magazines published in Japan. Annual sales run at around half a billion volumes. The circulation of some comic magazines is astonishing. In 1985 the popular *Shōnen Jump* broke all previous records for any weekly magazine with its run of 4,000,000. Most comic strips are long-term serials, first appearing in weekly or monthly magazines, then published in handy pocket-size soft cover editions. Some serial strips continue for years, running into multivolume works. The record breaker may well be Saitō Takao's *Golgo 13,* the story of a professional killer, Duke Togo, who travels around the world gunning down victims on contract. It has been running since 1969. Not untypical is the more benign *Notari Matsutarō,* Chiba Tetsuya's saga of an aspiring sumo wrestler, now in its twenty-second volume.

There are several thousand comic strip artists at work in Japan today. The most successful are rich and famous, often as well known as pop singers or pop journalists. They appear on television panel shows, their views on public issues are solicited, and their habits are grist for magazine and television feature stories. American youths may dream of making it on Broadway or in Hollywood, but many young Japanese, women as well as men, aspire to fame as comic strip artists. In 1986–87 NHK, the national television corporation, ran an evening drama, *Manga no michi,* about two friends who come to Tokyo from the provinces in the early 1950s to become professional cartoonists. It proved to be extremely popular, and, as you might guess, a hardback comic strip version of the story is available in the bookstores.

Comic strip artists are not only popular; they receive recognition from the literary establishment. In the United States the first comic strip artist ever to win a Pulitzer Prize was Garry Trudeau, author of the highly political and often controversial strip *Doonesbury*. The earlier winners have all been editorial cartoonists, whose seriousness of purpose validated their respectability. In Japan, on the other hand, annual literary prizes for comics are offered by major publishing houses like Kodansha and Bungeishunjusha. The comic strip is regarded as a literary form worthy of serious critical evaluation.

Two generations ago this was not the case. The comic strip was neither a widely popular media form nor a particularly respectable one. It had been introduced to Japan at the turn of the century by Kitazawa Rakuten, an illustrator and political cartoonist for Fukazawa Yukichi's *Jiji shinpō*. Inspired by the model of early American newspaper strips, Kitazawa began drawing a cartoon Sunday supplement for the paper, and in 1902, he introduced a humorous four-panel strip, *Tagosaku to Mokubei no Tōkyō kenbutsu*, about the misadventures of two country bumpkins in Tokyo. The narrative comic strip, likewise drawing on the American example, made its appearance in 1923 with the serialization of *Shōchan no boken* in the *Asahigraph*.

The comic strip never established a strong foothold in the Japanese newspaper. In the United States the Sunday funnies had become so popular by the 1930s that Fiorella LaGuardia, the mayor of New York, went on the radio during a major newspaper strike to read them to his constituents' children. In Japan, however, the comic narrative strip found another vehicle, the monthly children's magazine. Serialized narratives would first appear in monthlies like *Shōnen Club*, then as separate hardbound volumes in bookstores. One of the most successful strips, *Norakuro*, about a lovable stray dog who looked a little like Felix the Cat in canine drag, remains an icon of 1930s nostalgia, and a full edition of the series was recently republished. But until the end of World War II, comic strips were for children not for adults, and their readers were primary school students not university students or young office workers.

All this began to change after 1945. In the wake of defeat, the Japanese population, living in the ruins of its old dreams, was hungry for new ones. In the cities where daily life was a desperate scramble to keep food on the table and clothing on the back, there was an audience ready for escape from dreary reality to a world of fantasy, adventure, and romance. While the culture of the intellectual elite—the "Iwami" culture of the general and critical monthly magazines—was swept up in debates over "peace," "democracy," and "feudalism," mass culture was called on to answer a deep yearning for cheap and accessible escape. For adults movies provided such escape, and for children the comics did.

Comic pictures and comic strips became available in a variety and an abundance unknown before the war. *Kami shibai* (paper play) performers, traveling to family neighborhoods in the afternoon, narrated adventure stories illustrated by colorful cartoon drawings shown in a box mounted on the back of a bicycle. Many comic artists managed to make a living in the immediate postwar years by drawing for *kami shibai*. Others wrote strips for "red books," small cheap comic books printed on rough pulp paper, not unlike the Big Little Books so popular in the States during the 1930s and 1940s. But new boys' magazines like *Shōnen* and *Manga shōnen* gave the biggest boost to the spread of comic strips. In the manner of boys' literary magazines in the mid-Meiji period, *Manga shōnen* even solicited contributions from its readers and published the best of them. By the 1950s neighborhood lending libraries, where one could borrow a book or a comic for a few yen, became hangouts for children on their way from school.

The pivotal figure in the postwar revival of the narrative comic strip was Tezuka Osamu, known today as the "god of comics" (*manga no kamisama*). Tezuka had been an avid reader of *Norakuro* as a child, and he often helped his father, a Sumitomo executive, on his excursions as a Sunday painter. While studying at medical school in Osaka, he began drawing for local newspapers and for "red book" publishers. In March 1947 he brought out the first postwar comic best-seller, *Shintakarajima* (*New Treasure Island*), which sold 300,000–400,000 copies. In the years that followed he brought out other long strips now regarded as classics of the form—*Lost World, Metropolis, Jungle Taitei,* and *Tetsuwan Atomu.* (The last of these will be familiar to some American readers as *Astro Boy,* an animated cartoon based on Tezuka's strip that appeared on American television in the 1960s.) Eventually Tezuka left Osaka for a rundown apartment house in the suburbs of Tokyo, the Tokiwaso, where he became a magnet for aspiring comic strip artists, including Ishinomori Shōtarō, the author of this book.

The publication of *Shintakarajima* in 1947 marked the beginning of a revolution in the visual techniques of the narrative comic strip. In a sense Tezuka wedded the comic strip to the movie. He introduced cinematic techniques into his drawings, breaking away from the convention of presenting the action as though seen through a proscenium arch. His narrative eye was mobile, and readers watched his stories unfold as they would a movie. The opening of *Shintakarajima* took two pages and four frames to show the young hero setting down the road to adventure in open-top car. As Tezuka later observed, "Most [comic strips] were drawn . . . as if seated in an audience viewing a stage, where the actors emerge and interact. This made it impossible to create dramatic or psychological effects so I began to use cinematic techniques. Instead of using only one frame for an action or the climax (as was customary), I made a point of depicting a movement or facial expression with many frames and even many pages."

Japanese comic strips today have elaborated and refined this innovation, creating a distinctive visual code. Close-ups, varied viewing angles, stop-frame techniques, and visual sound effects create action sequences that often seem to leap out of the panel and off the page. In contrast to the American comic strip, crowded with dialogue balloons, the Japanese comic strip is a much more graphic form. The reader absorbs as much from the pictures as from the scanty text. Some comic strips run on for pages with no dialogue at all, interrupted only by the occasional grunt, gasp, shriek, sigh, or squish.

Coming from a middle-class background, Tezuka aspired to turn the comic strip into a respectable art form. He wanted to produce comic narratives that would rival the best children's literature. The selection of his title— *New Treasure Island*—was not coincidental. The book ran two hundred pages, and some of his later strips were many times as long. Length allowed Tezuka to introduce new complexity and continuity into his plots and to create characters with more depth and range of feeling. He transformed the narrative strip from a chronicle of pratfalls and adventures into a fictive world where characters experienced human feelings immediately recognizable to the child— sadness, fear, anger, and self-sacrifice as well as joy, courage and triumph.

What Tezuka did for boys' adventure, detective, and science fiction stories, others began to do for more adult themes. The mainstream comic narrative in Japan today is the *gekiga*—the dramatic picture story—drawn for the late adolescent or young adult audience. The first *gekiga* appeared in the late 1950s as the postwar generation of children readers grew into young adulthood. No longer interested in animals and robots, they demanded more substantial fare, and publishers responded to their change in taste.

One of the trailblazers was Shirato Sanpei's serial *Ninja bugeichō*, published in seventeen separate volumes between 1959 and 1962. Shirato introduced a new realism into his drawing, abandoning such conventions as four-fingered hands and Mickey Mouse eyes. He also introduced a new degree of "social realism" into his stories. The protagonist of *Ninja bugeichō* was Kagemaru, the leader of a *ninja* band, who fought on the side of rebellious peasants in the wars of the late sixteenth century. While the strip could be read as pure adventure, with swordfights and battles, at another level it was the story of the struggle of the oppressed against their feudal masters. It depicted a society in chaos, where death, destruction, and betrayal flourished. The moral message was complex. Kagemaru was not so much superhero as antihero. Although in the end he is defeated by the entrenched powers-that-be, the strip suggested that struggle itself was of value, whatever its immediate outcome. When one remembers that the strip appeared at the time of the unsuccessful demonstrations against the Japanese-U.S. Mutual Security Treaty, its popularity among student and young adult readers is understandable.

The development of the *gekiga* paralleled the diffusion of television in Japan. In 1958 less than 20 percent of Japanese households owned television sets; by 1968 nearly 100 percent did. A whole generation grew up accustomed to absorbing as much information, entertainment, and ideas from the picture tube as from the printed page. And as income levels rose with the rapid expansion of the economy, so did disposable income in the hands of children, adolescents, and young adults. No longer did readers of comics have to borrow dog-eared volumes from the neighborhood lending library.

Large publishing companies realized that the market for comic books and comic magazines was growing, and the comic industry rode the middle-class consumer revolution of the 1960s just as the appliance, electronic, and automobile industries did. The publication of comic magazines shifted from a monthly to a weekly schedule, their number proliferated, and their circulation shot upward. In 1966 a single issue of *Shōnen* magazine broke the million mark. It was no longer possible to dismiss the comic strip as kid stuff. Strips about cute robots and cuddly animals continued to appear, but so did those about nihilistic samurai swordsmen, wartime soldiers, high school gangs, kamikaze pilots, harried office workers, gangsters and *yakuza,* occult superheroes, champion mah-jongg players, and so on, and so on, and so on.

One popular genre of *gekiga* was the sports comic strip. These were uplifting narratives about ambitious and determined youths—and occasionally young women—who fought their way from obscurity to the championship (or its equivalent) in judo, baseball, sumo, soccer, karate, horseracing, boxing, tennis, or almost any sport one can imagine. *Kyōjin no hoshi,* a popular strip appearing between 1966 and 1971, told the story of Hoshi Hyuma, the son of a former baseball player, ruthlessly trained by his father for the big leagues. Hoshi eventually becomes the star pitcher for the Giants, then the Japanese equivalent of the New York Yankees, only to injure his arm in a climactic game with his main rival, an American pitcher, also trained by his father. Although the sadomasochistic element (to say nothing of the oedipal) of sports strips is obvious enough, so is their character-building didactic. The central theme is the importance of *konjō* (spirit). Their heroes succeed by dint of hard work, self-denial, abstinence, dedication, persistence, manliness, and pluck, precisely the virtues needed in the high school student's struggle to succeed in university examinations or in the ambitious young office worker's climb up the corporate ladder.

Another *gekiga* genre emerging in the 1970s was the "young girls' comic" aimed at adolescent girls or unmarried young women. In these strips, delicate heroines with (literally) shining eyes flutter their improbably long lashes over androgynous male characters who are superhuman models of gentleness and sensitivity. While the sports comics focused on male striving for success and excellence, girl's strips dealt with sublimated erotic female fantasies. Their usual themes were the fulfillment of romantic yearnings, the requiting of impossible love, and the union of sympathetic souls. Impossibly saccharine at times, they resembled the Takarazuka musicals so popular among Japanese girls, where all-female casts costumed in hoop skirts and hussar uniforms sing and dance their way through sappy love stories. The didactic element, of course, is not absent in these strips either. Their readers are not likely to become feminists. They learn that if women are soft, passive, and willing to sacrifice all for their man they will find fulfillment. In a society where real men cry only when they win (or lose) the championship, that is a useful message.

It was perhaps inevitable that the *gekiga* become a vehicle for pedagogy as well as entertainment. By the middle of the 1980s the "study comic" (*benkyō manga*) and the "practical comic" (*jitsumu manga*) had made their appearance. Publishers produced comic strip textbooks for school children explaining mathematics or physics and multivolume comic strip histories of Japan, China, and even the world. Securities companies began to put out comic strip brochures unraveling the complications of investment in the stock market, and even the political parties tried to reach the growing army of indifferent young voters by explaining their policies in comic books. The young adult audience, which has become used to eating in fast-food chains and shopping at 24-hour convenience stores, has found the how-to-do-it comic book a quick and handy way to learn about legal problems, adult diseases, office etiquette, personal computers, tourism abroad, and other useful subjects.

The present volume marks the arrival of the pedagogical or educational comic strip at a new level of sophistication. Its author, Ishinomori (formerly Ishimori) Shōtarō, is one of Japan's all-star comic strip artists, a prodigiously productive worker who sometimes draws two hundred or three hundred pages per month. As a middle school student Ishinomori became a disciple of Tezuka Osamu, and while still in high school he published his first strip as a contributor to *Shōnen manga*. His range of work has been remarkable. He has drawn children's stories, science fiction, and even girls' comics. It was reported in 1980 that after twenty-five years as a comic strip artist he had drawn 70,000 pages and published 367 separate volumes. Ishimori is best known for two strips—*Cyborg 009*, about an international band of artificial humans who struggle to prevent the evil Black Ghost Gang from taking over the world, and *Ichi torimono hikae*, a detective series set in the late Edo period.

The Japanese version of *Japan Inc.*—*Manga Nihon keizai nyūmon*—was published in late 1986 by the *Nihon keizai shimbun*, the Japanese equivalent of the *Wall Street Journal*. It is based on *Zeminaru Nihon keizai nyūmon*, a serious introductory economics text put out by the paper. As Ishinomori told one reporter, "If people don't understand [the book], they can read the comic version to understand complicated issues easily and quickly while having fun." The volume brings complex issues, facts, and figures into focus by personalizing and dramatizing them, and not surprisingly it became an instant best seller. Over 550,000 copies were sold in less than a year.

Like most Japanese comics (*Cyborg 009*, for example) this one presents the reader with an ensemble of prototypical characters. With appropriate costume changes they would not be out of place in a samurai, sports, or science fiction strip. All of them work for Mitsutomo Trading Company, the kind of general trading company that has presided over Japan's external economic expansion during the past century. Kudō, the young office worker, stands for honesty, fairness, and social responsibility in business; Tsugawa, his foil, is an ambitious careerist willing to stop at nothing to advance his own fortunes and those of the company; Akiyama, an older version of Kudō, offers his young protégé counsel and tries to keep company policy on the right track; Toda, an older version of Tsugawa, always backs his devious schemes; Amamiya, a feisty young OL (office lady), worships Kudō from afar; and Ueda, the bumbling office assistant straight from the countryside, is goofy over Amamiya and anxious to succeed but not quite sure whether to imitate Kudō or Tsugawa.

These characters are led through six episodes dealing with recent changes in the Japanese economy—trade friction with the United States, the appreciation of the yen, the impact of rising oil prices, the financing of government debt through the issue of government bonds, the internationalization of business and banking, and the adjustment of the domestic markets to new consumer tastes. While the book gives an obligatory nod to sex and violence—after all there are certain expectations about adult comic strips in Japan—its tone is serious in the main. The reader is bombarded with charts showing the movement of exchange rates or the composition of the budget, side notes on the Smithsonian Agreement or the Euroyen, and quotations from economic wise men ranging from Adam Smith to Paul Samuelson. When the attentive reader has finished, he should know a great deal more about the Japanese economy than when he began. He can also learn a great deal about how the Japanese view their political economy.

In the recent and much heralded "revolution" in the American comic strip, superheroes have been reduced to human proportions. Superman now has neurotic flaws. Perhaps that tells something about the state of the American national psyche in the twilight of its hegemonic era. This book tells us even more about the national mood in Japan, where apprehension and optimism jostle one another as the country heads toward what some predict will be "the Japanese century."

American readers, accustomed to media coverage emphasizing the strengths and achievements of the Japanese economy, may be surprised at this book's emphasis on Japan's economic problems and vulnerability. Many Japanese, even comic strip artists, see Japan as a beleaguered economy, weak in resources and dependent on the outside world for survival. As one of Ishinomori's colleagues observed in a recent newspaper interview, "I feel it's a wonder that Japan has grown to this point economically. Japan, you could say, is a mansion built on sand, without any resources at all, and depending on human brains." A sense of national self-pity, undoubtedly nurtured by unrelenting struggle to catch up with the Western economies and by memories of wartime and postwar devastation, has been one of the principal psychological underpinnings of Japan's postwar economic achievements. It has also made Japanese sensitive to what they see as unfair and vindictive attitudes of foreigners, not all of them Americans necessarily, who resent these achievements.

The book also reflects a deep suspicion of politicians and bureaucrats, often the very people American writers identify as the principal agents of the "Japanese miracle." The business of politicians, it would seem from reading this book, is private gain not public interest. The prime minister, a thinly disguised version of the then-incumbent, Nakasone Yasuhiro, appears more worried about his government's popularity than about taking the right economic course. In one episode he decides to sacrifice sound national financial policy in order to keep his party's supporters happy before an election. When at the last moment he seems concerned that this might lead to inflation, a mysterious shadowy adviser tells him not to worry: "If

necessary we can always lie. That's politics." The distrust of authority is a
perennial theme in the Japanese comic strip, especially the "lone samurai"
strips, but the political cynicism in this book undoubtedly reflects political
apathy among young voters who regard party politics as a struggle for
position and power that has little to do with their lives.

In the final analysis, the message of the book is that the success of
the Japanese economy will not depend on resource endowments or political
management but on business practices that are ethical, socially responsible,
and forward-looking. The message is conveyed by the struggle between Kudō
and Tsugawa over company policy and, by implication, over business
morality. Tsugawa, the aggressive go-getter, is the archetypical profit
maximizer, willing to use any method, fair or foul, honest or dishonest, to get
ahead. He is indifferent to the impact of company policies on the lives of
others—or even his own. Kudō, on the other hand, is always mindful of the
little people—the subcontractors hurt by the shift of automobile production
facilities off shore, the people of the provincial shipbuilding city hard hit by
the fall-off in demand for merchant vessels, the old people warehoused in a
glittery but indifferent retirement home, and the farmers whose way of life will
be destroyed by the opening of the agricultural market. He urges taking the
long view, and he is suspicious of policies aimed at paper profits rather than
the production and marketing of good and useful products. As his mentor
Akiyama says: "We must have money for our real purpose—to make and sell
good products—but it's stupid to run a business to raise profits simply by
moving money around." In other words, the social utility of business is as
important as its profitability.

Shibusawa Eiichi, the grand old moralist of the Meiji business world,
would have recognized the message. The idea that businessmen should
concern themselves as much with the wider community as with the bottom
line is a durable theme in the folklore of modern Japanese capitalism. Just as
the Meiji businessman was wont to claim that he was working for "the profit
of the nation" rather than personal gain—even as the dividends came rolling in
—postwar business leaders often describe themselves as custodians of the
common good. In 1956, on the eve of the postwar takeoff, the *Keizai dōyūkai*
announced that "enterprises can no longer be looked at as something entrusted
to management by the suppliers of capital alone; they are also entrusted by
society at large." Other business organizations quickly subscribed to this
rhetoric. Although industrial pollution in the 1950s and 1960s demonstrated
this philosophy was often more honored in the breach than in the custom, its
persistent appeal to Japanese managers is undeniable, and it is no wonder that

we find it as the moral matrix for a best-selling comic book on the Japanese economy.

A second volume of *Manga Nihon keizai nyūmon* has already appeared, perhaps the beginning of a series that will stretch into the "Japanese century." It is interesting to note, however, that the hero and heroine of the new volume, while they are Japanese working for Japanese banks, are both graduates of Harvard Business School. That may provide a more reliable prognosis of the future of Japanese-American economic relations than statistics on the popularity of comic books among Japanese and American high school students.

Peter Duus
Stanford University

1

Trade Friction

Under a system of perfectly free commerce, each country naturally
devotes its capital and labor to such employments as are most
beneficial to each. This pursuit of individual advantage is admirably
connected with the universal good of the whole. By stimulating
industry, by rewarding ingenuity, and by using most efficaciously the
peculiar powers bestowed by nature, it distributes labour most
effectively and most economically: while, by increasing the general
mass of productions, it diffuses general benefit, and binds together by
one common tie of interest and intercourse, the universal society of
nations throughout the civilized world.

David Ricardo, *Principles of Political Economy and Taxation*

IN WHICH we see how international trade friction grates on the affairs of the Toyosan Automobile Corporation and its affiliate, the Mitsutomo Company:

U.S. automobile interests force Japanese companies to restrict the export of cars, and Toyosan's president decides to move production to the U.S.;

Mitsutomo's wily Tsugawa is called upon to eradicate union opposition to the move and facilitate the takeover of a plant in the U.S.;

Toyosan's union leader Sato discovers that his personal predilections and political ambitions prevent the pursuit of union interests;

and Mitsutomo's kind-hearted Kudo learns much about earlier trade-friction crises, but is unable to save the Japanese subcontractors who have been manufacturing parts for Toyosan cars.

After the second oil crisis, sales of gas-saving Japanese cars took off in the U.S. In 1980 there was a recorded growth of 17.6% over 1979, and automobile friction rose.

The U.S. trade balance took a turn for the worse in the middle of the 1960s. Beginning in the 1970s, the deficit came to stay; the gap increased every year, reaching $148.4 billion in 1985.

8

The U.S. trade deficit with Japan was less than $2 billion in the early 1970s. In the late 1970s, it increased to nearly $10 billion; in 1985, to nearly $50 billion.

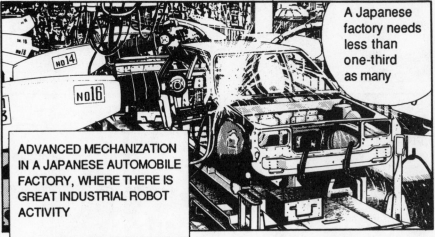

ADVANCED MECHANIZATION IN A JAPANESE AUTOMOBILE FACTORY, WHERE THERE IS GREAT INDUSTRIAL ROBOT ACTIVITY

The U.S. produced about 11,480,000 cars in 1979. In 1982 production fell below 7,000,000. Japan became the world's top manufacturer of cars in 1980, and the U.S. had to be content with second place.

Analysts say that the U.S. lost its place as king of the car makers because it failed to update its equipment and because it has not put its efforts into production.

The U.S. plays up the claim that 500,000 workers are unemployed because of Japanese car imports. Others have suggested, however, that if the U.S. mechanized and rationalized like Japan, that change would produce about 400,000 unemployed workers (Omae Ken'ichi, *The World Appears, Japan Appears*).

Half of all U.S. exports to Japan are foodstuffs and raw materials; the U.S. imports mainly machinery and vehicle parts from Japan. This pattern is typical of trade between developing and advanced nations — with the U.S. playing the part of the developing nation.

You can trust me

e, keep noses an

TOYOSAN

TOYOSAN
SIX MONTHS LATER

AT THE MAIN OFFICE
OF THE MITSUTOMO COMPANY

Next year's estimate is for 1.68 million cars

That won't shake up the business world

Hmmm. Even the government can't hold out any longer

Self-restriction of automobile exports began at 1.68 million per year during the period from 1981 to 1983. Exports rose to 1.85 million in 1984 and to 2.30 million in 1985 and 1986.

Self-restriction controlled 40% of Japanese exports to the U.S. Proponents of free trade would say that this was indisputably a step backward.

According to statistics, when a country's income level rises, so does its demand for Japanese products. Japan's particular strength is in industries that produce goods for markets with high income elasticity.

Another point of friction is semiconductors. In the U.S.-Japanese semiconductor trade, the balance went in favor of Japan for the first time in 1980. Problems set in immediately; they were temporarily resolved by a reciprocal lowering of tariffs.

Changes in Trade Friction

Postwar trade friction with Japan has had three peaks.

The first, a dispute over textiles, lasted from 1968 to 1972. The second, in the late 1970s, centered on iron and steel and color TVs. The third, from 1980 to the present, focuses on automobiles, semiconductors, and communications equipment.

During the first period, Japan greatly increased its exports by using its weapon of cheap labor to achieve superiority in value. Now Japan is being exposed to similar aggression by other Asian nations.

During the second period, Japan saturated the U. S. market with its goods, using not only cheap labor but also high productivity and efficient products to achieve technical superiority.

In the third period, cheap labor is no longer an issue. The main factors are entirely technical, focusing on technological development and management of goods. The trade battlefield has moved to areas of high technical intensity. This trend seems to be growing stronger, as signs appear of "high-tech" friction in advanced fields. Because these fields are closely connected to national security, the U. S. responses are different from its earlier ones.

Recent Trade Friction Incidents

Between Japan and the U. S.

1981	Δ Japan began self-restriction of automobile exports to the U. S. (1981-1983)
1982	Δ When the U. S. opened its large-scale photo-communications system to public bidding, Fujitsu placed the highest bid, but the U. S. rejected it.
	Δ U. S. iron and steel companies sued Japanese iron and steel producers for unfair trading practices.
1983	Δ The U. S. sharply raised its tariff on motorcycles of over 700 cc.
	Δ Agreements between Japan and the U. S. about self-restriction of automobile exports were extended to 1984.
	Δ The U. S. demanded that Japan open its money and stock markets.
1984	Δ Japan greatly increased its imports of U. S. beef and oranges.
	Δ Japan proposed a program to gradually open its money and stock markets.
1985	Δ Japan decided on an "action program" to open its markets (to the world).

Between Japan and Europe

1981	Δ A meeting of the European Community (EC) decided to monitor imports from Japan of automobiles and NC (numerical control) construction machinery.
1982	Δ The EC meeting decided to discuss the place of Japanese trade policy in GATT (General Tariff and Trade Pact).
	Δ France centralized the customs clearance of all VTRs (video tape recorders) at the inland city of Poitiers.
1983	Δ A meeting of the EC demanded Japanese self-restriction of 10 Japanese-made items, including VTRs and color TVs.
	Δ France introduced a prior notification system for the importation of 6 items, including construction machinery.
	Δ A meeting of the EC raised the tariff on DADs (digital audio discs).
1984	Δ A meeting of the EC demanded that Japan encourage imports and ease up on exports.
1985	Δ The first meeting was held of the Japanese-EC Committee on the Expansion of Trade.

A country's custom statistics form the basis for its export statistics. But the standards for the statistics are different in the U.S. and in Japan. The figures announced by Japan for its trade surplus with the U.S. and those announced by the U.S. for its trade deficit with Japan do not agree.

THE HOME OF TOYOSAN'S MANAGING DIRECTOR

Japan's export elasticity (Japan's increase in exports compared to the growth rat previous exports) is 1.717. That means that exports are increasing at a rate 1.71 times the world rate.

VAROOM!

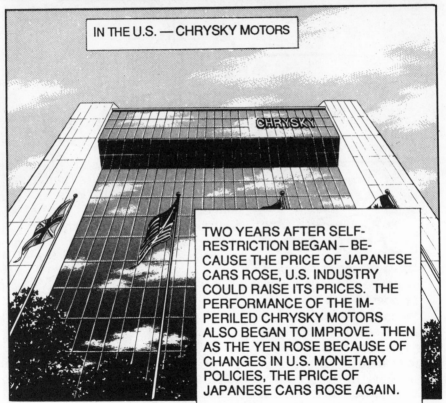

IN THE U.S. — CHRYSKY MOTORS

TWO YEARS AFTER SELF-RESTRICTION BEGAN — BECAUSE THE PRICE OF JAPANESE CARS ROSE, U.S. INDUSTRY COULD RAISE ITS PRICES. THE PERFORMANCE OF THE IMPERILED CHRYSKY MOTORS ALSO BEGAN TO IMPROVE. THEN AS THE YEN ROSE BECAUSE OF CHANGES IN U.S. MONETARY POLICIES, THE PRICE OF JAPANESE CARS ROSE AGAIN.

... for these reasons I think we are justified in saying that the company is completely out of danger

The competition with Japan has been hard, but now we have nothing to fear

Up to now, Japan has profited from unjust exchange rates and long-term labor and government protection, but now the country has had to change because of international criticism

Above all, the dollar-yen exchange rate is approaching a proper level. It is weakening the competitiveness of Japanese cars. In time it will create conditions where their companies will have to move into local U.S. production

In order to still foreign criticism, the Japanese government adopted an "action program." Its central points were the lowering of duties on 1,853 goods and the simplification of standards, certification, and import procedures.

26

Japanese import elasticity is extremely low: 0.742. Even if Japanese income increases, imports increase very little. Only in Japan does export elasticity exceed import elasticity.

From 1971 to 1976 Japan's direct overseas investment averaged 40.2% from 1971 to 1976; from 1976 to 1983 it increased by 17.9%. Recently, however, many companies have changed from exporting to overseas manufacturing.

Don't worry about money or methods

How you do it is up to you. I'm only worried about our cover being broken. Please be careful about that

because we're in this together

I gotcha ... he he he

Sato wants to run for the Diet with union backing

Get hold of a scandal about him! Make one up!

Oh boy!

Now it's really heating up, isn't it!

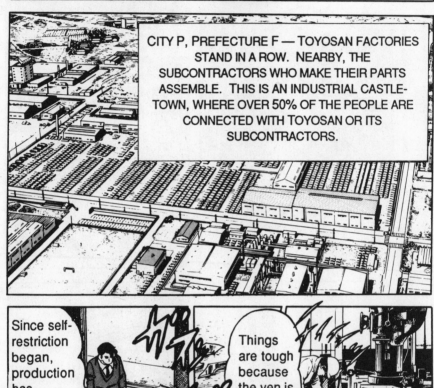

CITY P, PREFECTURE F — TOYOSAN FACTORIES STAND IN A ROW. NEARBY, THE SUBCONTRACTORS WHO MAKE THEIR PARTS ASSEMBLE. THIS IS AN INDUSTRIAL CASTLE-TOWN, WHERE OVER 50% OF THE PEOPLE ARE CONNECTED WITH TOYOSAN OR ITS SUBCONTRACTORS.

In the U.S. in 1983, a "local contents" law reappeared, which required manufacturers selling over 100,000 passenger cars a year to use a proportion of American-made parts, set according to the number of cars they sold.

Mr. Kudo! For the subcontractors this is a matter of life and death!

...

Can't Mitsutomo create new jobs for us?

Something besides car parts ... ?

Japan restricts 23 imports: 22 agricultural products and coal. This is a small number compared to France's 46, but it is large compared to the U.S.'s 7, England's 3, and West Germany's 4. It is a source of foreign criticism of Japan.

The Hollowing Out of Industry

When the exchange rate reaches ¥150 to $1, Japanese industry begins to actively encourage overseas expansion. Except in the field of automobiles, when $1 reaches the ¥150 level, labor costs per hour become cheaper in the U. S. than in Japan.

Rather than manufacture in Japan and export to the U. S., it becomes cheaper to build factories in the U. S. and manufacture and sell products there. As the yen continues to rise, it is even possible that Nissan or Toyota automobiles made in the U. S. will be shipped to Japan.

If this is the case in the U. S., where labor costs are high, it is even truer in Korea and the NICs (newly industrialized countries) of Southeast Asia.

Therefore, it is becoming common for industries to move their bases overseas in order to reduce manufacturing costs. There is concern that, as this trend continues, it will bring about a decline in employment in Japan.

In 1986, 94% of the companies replying to an Economics Association survey said that they "expected the international decentralization of their home company to be even greater in the future." In addition, according to the Japanese Data Development Center, employment was lower in 41 out of 48 categories of industries; a decline in employment of 900,000 was predicted for the next 50 years.

The development of direct overseas investment and the concomitant shrinking of manufacture within Japan is known as "hollowing out."

The phrase "hollowing out of industry" was first used to describe the U. S. as business capital fled overseas to escape the domestic aging of capital stock brought about by high interest rates and the rise of the dollar. As a result, factory after factory closed down. As manufacturing in the U. S. continued to shrink, part of the surplus workforce was absorbed into service industries, but unemployment increased, creating deep social problems.

Japan will not necessarily fall into the predicament of the U. S., but many observers feel that Japan, with its small domestic market, could find itself in an equally serious situation.

When $1 = ¥ 150, Labor Costs Are Cheaper in the U.S. (Except Cars)

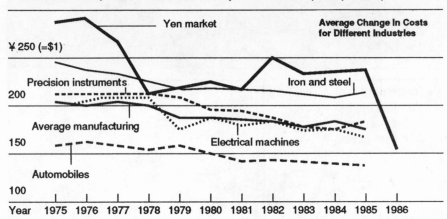

Note: The same standard has been used for Japanese and U.S. wage costs and hourly wage costs.

An import surcharge is an additional tax levied on imports in order to restrain them. In the European Community, when imported agricultural products from outside a region are lower in price than the region's products, the difference is collected in an import surcharge.

Kudo, how did you make out?

Sir?

I wanted to know how Toyosan was going to supply parts to its plants in the U.S.

Mainly I wanted to learn what the subcontractors should do

And … what did you decide?

During the trade friction over color TVs, Japanese manufacturers all began to set up local U.S. factories

As a result, almost no color TVs were exported to the U.S.

Electrical appliance manufacturers moved everything abroad, including their parts divisions

The subcontractors that were left behind came through with no problem

In 1985 U.S. Senator John Claggett Danforth introduced legislation to correct the imbalance in U.S.-Japanese trade that has been called the "Revenge-Against-Japan Act." The Senate has adopted a wait-and-see attitude about it.

Leave that to me

I've already started working on it ... it should be settled soon

Oh?

You seem sure of yourself

I am

Really? Well ... don't get

your fingers burned

...

THE BLACK ROSE

he he ... that bastard!

A little S&M to relieve his stress, huh!

I've finally caught him in the act

You don't give up, do you!

No matter how often you come, I'll deny everything

Do me a favor?

Play dumb

about me coming here

Besides customs duties, the main restraints on imports are non-tariff barriers. The U.S. has criticized the Japanese government's method of licensing and its administrative actions, the organization of the Japanese enterprise system, and the Japanese insistence on the superiority of its products.

A private advisory group, the Economic Structure Coordinating Committee, has urged the prime minister to move toward domestic-demand economics. It has put together the Maekawa Report, which advocates a comprehensive residential policy, a reform of the tariff system, and an expansion of agricultural imports.

My customers are all top executives and famous or cultured people

You'd never know that they go in for sex in the afternoon

They're people like that?

People like that!

And what about you? What about a little "S" this evening?

I can really give it to you

ERG!

Don't make jokes like that! I'm absolutely normal!

ha ha ha

I'll call you soon

Hello ... Tsugawa?

I got it all

on ultra-sensitive film

Another focus of friction is in the area of the trade of services rather than goods. Japan is being pressed to liberalize its money and securities practices, the strong U.S. areas.

It's much more efficient than buying land, building a plant, and getting together your own workforce

Uh huh

Now that U.S. farms are in a slump, stock in farm machinery companies is cheap. But ...

for strangers — and Japanese besides — to suddenly take over management ...

will local workers be willing to work for them?

Mmm ... it's a big problem

But over there, company owners change all the time

Mama! If this shop suddenly got a new owner, what would you do? Would you quit?

What? You mean out of the blue?

Uh huh. That's the way the new manager works

...

Well, it'd be fine if he was as understanding as Mr. Akiyama

But if he was mean, I'd leave pretty fast,

'cause I've still got plenty of guys on the string

ha ha ha

The workers would probably feel the same way

... The other problem is the sub-contractors

If the factories move to the U.S., people are going to be left behind — it's going to cause anxiety.

Umh

...

If we could only find some sort of solution

In 1984 the Japanese-American Yen-Dollar Committee discussed problems of the money and capital markets, seeking agreement on the right of foreign securities companies (including the trust divisions of foreign banks) to buy seats on the Tokyo Stock Exchange.

One point of contention between the U.S. and Japan involves supplying materials to the telephone company (NTT). The U.S.'s assertion that the company's doors are closed to U.S. firms has remained a sore point.

In discussing the cost of trade, three statistics are used: FOB, CIF, and FAS. FOB (free on board) refers to the manufacturing cost and not the cost of transportation; CIT stands for cost, insurance, and freight; FAS (free alongside ship) means delivery at the side of the ship free of charges.

In 1985 Japan achieved a 5% economic growth; its greatest driving force was an expansion of exports. When this spawned trade friction, there were demands for change to an economy based on domestic demand.

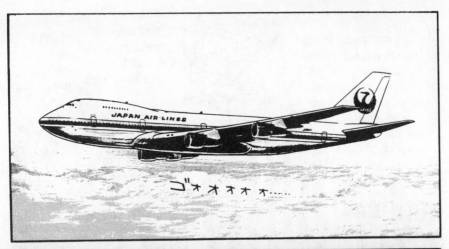

NEW YORK

Can't we buy them up so the market price won't change? Who would do the buying? It would be awkward if we were exposed

Well ... shall I try?

52

"Priority production industries" have traditionally been fostered by the Japanese government, but in the U.S. they are protected only in special areas such as the aerospace industry. The U.S. has criticized them as a kind of non-tariff barrier.

There's a rumor that union leader Sato made a deal to run for the Diet

The companies are money mad! The unions are mad for their own chance...

Nobody is thinking about our sub-contractors

...

...

Japan's elasticity of exports to the U.S. was about 4 times that of imports from the U.S. In effect, unless Japan grows at 4 times the speed of the U.S., trade and expenditures will not balance.

It's just like Tsugawa—this idea to take over the depressed farm-machinery plant

They settled for 1/10 the real value of the property

Isn't it high-handed to secretly buy up other people's companies?

I wonder how the people feel who work there

If you think about things like that, you can't do business

Those people probably decided that it's better to have jobs than to get fired

Is that so? Mr. Kudo's the fall guy again ... it's OK though,

if nothing goes wrong.

Farm Machi
Manufactu
NORTH CA

NORTH CAROLINA

When direct overseas investment is progressing, internal production shrinks and employment declines. This phenomenon is called "industrial hollowing out." The high value of the yen promotes overseas investment and brings about hollowing out.

he
he
he
Thanks
a lot

uh huh …
So Sato
has those
kinds of
tastes …

I still
have a
copy.
Want
me to
lend it
to you?

he
he
he

You mean
next time
you'll
blackmail
me?

Boy,
you're a
tough one!
ha ha ha

Mr. Kudo! We solved Toyosan's problem too! Let's celebrate!

A celebration is fine, Ueda, but actually the critical time for Toyosan's U.S. plant is from now on

That's right …it's settled … the plant is running properly and producing cars just like the ones made in Japan

How about that!

We'll be working beside people with different customs and different languages and different skin color

The Japanese tariff rate of 2.5 % (1983) is low compared to the U.S.'s 3.6% and the European Community's 2.7 %. In terms of tariffs, Japan can be considered the star pupil.

Well, I don't care where I work or who I work with

Yankee women aren't bad either

hmmm … I'll never understand your generation

…

That's because he's an alien!

Huh?

Hey! That's going too far!

But … Kudo, I have a feeling that once more events are going to revolve around you!

!

Hey! You mean it's going to be Mr. Kudo's problem again?!

Mr. Tsugawa started it! He should finish it!

I knew it! You're on Kudo's side!

Trade friction means that Japanese products become a problem for other countries. Reverse trade friction means that Japan has begun to be pursued by the middle advanced nations in areas such as textiles, chemical products, iron and steel, and electrical products.

2

Countering the Rise of the Yen

The price of the dollar, if determined freely, serves the same function all other prices. It transmits information and provides an incentive to act on that information because it affects the incomes that participants in the market receive.

Milton Friedman, *Free to Choose*

IN WHICH we see how changes in the international exchange rate cause the value of the yen to soar and Japanese bankruptcies to skyrocket:

the plummeting finances of companies in the export center of Imahama attract the wily Tsugawa, who sees a chance to buy land cheaply and build a Mitsutomo-operated amusement park;

Imahama's mayor seeks assistance from outside and discovers the indifference of government and the strength of hometown ties;

the kind-hearted Kudo renews an old relationship in an effort to save the employees of Imahama's endangered companies;

and Boss Shijima demonstrates the power of both his personal loyalty and his political clout as he provides an enlightened alternative to Mitsutomo's amusement park.

The exchange rate should be thought of as the price of currency. If a dollar that could be bought for ¥200 comes to be bought for only ¥180, the yen has increased in va

By the way ... what did that young whippersnapper say?

Tsugawa?

About the company land? Sell it or sell out or ...

HMPH!

That pipsqueak is laughing at us! We're failing, but ...

I'll be damned if we'll be crushed!!

Tomorrow you have a conference with the subcontractors don't you?

Yes.

... It's tough ...

We've already cut costs as much as we can

With a high yen, when export industries change export charges from dollars to yen, the net profit decreases and they suffer a loss. Therefore, export industries generally lose money when the yen is high and import industries make a profit.

A major spinning company, Yamato Spinning, closed its plant in Saga on March 25, 1986. Founded in 1916, it had manufactured cotton thread and cloth for 70 years, but it was floored by the high yen.

... Well, I'm off to Mitsuaki Real Estate. See you later!

Uh huh ... ...

DEPARTMENT HEAD

... ...

Hey! Did you know we had these papers?

Hello Operations Department

In March 1986 Daimaru Department Store began to sell blouses and skirts made in Thailand. The same company made dress patterns and was a leading local industry; its prices were close to half the prices for the same kinds of goods made in Japan.

In the autumn of 1986, one year after the yen began to rise, the price of foreign-made urea fell to about one half. Because the price was about 40% of domestic urea's, Mitsubishi Oil and Chemical Company began to import urea made in Indonesia or Qatar.

VOOM

When did it start?

When did I begin to get annoyed at the sight of Kudo?

In the old days, it wasn't like that

We were always together

We were different types, but somehow we got along

When I married Reiko, he was as happy as if it was his own wedding

That was over 10 years ago ...

... Those were the days. But then Kudo and I changed ...

With the high yen, imports from NICs (newly industrialized countries) are increasing rapidly: manufacturing has suddenly increased in Japanese subsidiaries in NICs, where manufacturing costs are cheaper.

Certain makers of electrical products calculate that it becomes cheaper to manufacture in the U.S. when the exchange rate falls below ¥170 to $1.

You've changed ...

Changed ...

Ch ...

Sir!

Sir!

!

We're here ...

Hmmm ...

MITSUAKI REAL ESTATE

MINISTRY OF
TRADE AND INDUSTRY (MITI)

OFFICE OF THE VICE-MINISTER

The city is already at its last gasp …

Of course there are many, many things we would like to do

But … this year's subsidies and emergency funds have hit bottom …

VICE-MINISTER
KOBAYASHI

The electrical sector was hit directly by the rise in the yen; business suddenly worsened. In January 1986 Toshiba cut the salaries of its employees; in April Mitsubishi Electric Company froze salaries above department-head level.

Bottom?
But ...
um ...

Hmmm ...
well ...
let me
have a little
more time
...

It's because there is no more time that I've come to you

Mayor, it's my home town ... it's not that I'm not concerned, but ...

since I also work for the country, I'd like you to settle this problem

Oh! I'm sorry, but that's all for today ...

I have an important appointment

All right

He made me wait 3 hours ... to see him less than 10 minutes

I guess I have only Boss Shijima to rely on

When the G5 (the finance ministers of the U.S., England, Japan, West Germany, and France) met on September 22, 1985, to revise the dollar exchange rate, $1 was worth ¥242. One year later, on September 22, 1986, the market price was ¥153 to $1.

83

Japan imports 90% of its wheat, but during the recent high-yen period, wheat did not get any cheaper. Because of the government's policy to protect domestic wheat producers, the marginal profit went to the government.

THE PRIME MINISTER'S OFFICIAL RESIDENCE

PRIME MINISTER NAKANE

...

Well, well ...

It's difficult, isn't it

The exporters and the media criticize our measures to stop the rise of the yen as stopgap

And as you say, we have not taken any genuine steps … but we are also hindered by the mood of the cabinet

Well … Be patient a little longer … To make Japanese industry international, we should float until we reach ¥150 to $1

Then we can sail into economic revolution aboard the high yen, just as in 1868 we sailed into political revolution aboard the black ships from abroad

In September 1986, in order to ride out the high-yen recession, the Japanese government decided on comprehensive economic countermeasures. Even though the scale of business had been great in the past, because of the government's difficult financial situation, there were doubts about its effectiveness.

hmm ... even so, it's certainly a headache

hahaha ... that's not like you!

By the way, Mr. Prime Minister

Today there is a matter about which I wish to consult you

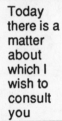

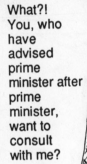

What?! You, who have advised prime minister after prime minister, want to consult with me?

...

Look upon it as the request of one who has left the world

...

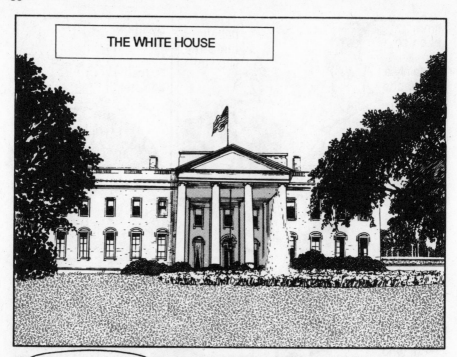

After April 1986, when the exchange rate topped ¥180 to $1, Japanese overseas industry increased sharply. There were many months when as many as 150 manufacturing companies rushed overseas.

The leading bearing company, Minebea, manufactures 95% of its tiny bearings in Thailand. After 1985, with the rise of the yen and the fall of the Thai currency, products imported into Japan became 50% cheaper and business competition increased.

In September 1986, a shadow was cast over the previously firm base number of exported cars and household electrical appliances. There was a great decline in store for profits because of the rise in the yen and the corresponding fall in production.

Let me tell you this ... My greatest concern is jobs!

If the unemployment rate goes down, we can win the next election easily

Huh?

Yes! In my state, because Toyosan has established a plant ...

Enough! I'm getting tired

So, I'll leave you ...

...

Japan imports 1.2 billion barrels of crude oil a year. In 1985, one barrel cost $28 and $1 equaled ¥250; in June 1986, $1 equaled ¥160. The marginal profit was ¥6 trillion.

When the yen goes up, unexpected customers drop in

Import-related enterprises such as electricity, gas, and oil profit from the rise in the yen. During one quarter in 1986, when the yen was high, the combined marginal profit of 12 oil companies was ¥164.6 billion. In the previous quarter, when the yen was low, the marginal loss was ¥38.3 billion.

The Forces That Move the Yen Market

When exports increase, the dollar becomes cheap on the foreign exchange because producers exchange the dollars they have received for yen. Operational profits increase from transactions involving tangible assets. Sales of dollars begin to exceed purchases of dollars; the dollar falls and the yen rises.

Capital income is an expression of transactions involving financial assets, such as lending and borrowing money or issuing bonds. If money flows overseas in excess of operational profits, then the yen will weaken.

Interest rates in the U. S. are high. Japanese investors seeking these high rates change yen into dollars. As they sell yen and buy dollars, they cause a fall in the yen and a rise in the dollar. And when U. S. prices rise because of inflation and Japanese prices are stable, the purchasing power of the dollar falls; the dollar falls and the yen rises.

The theory of purchasing power parity argues that differences in purchasing power determine the exchange rate. A Japanese and an American each buys the goods he needs. If the American pays $100 and the Japanese pays ¥15,000, in effect $1=¥150. This is an illustration of the theory of purchasing power parity.

According to the popular "bubble theory," money market rates are determined by market outlook, just as stock prices are. Even though a certain currency is relatively high in terms of economic fundamentals, if most markets expect its price to rise it will continue to rise. But if it strays too far from these fundamentals, it will burst like a soap bubble.

The pronouncements of politicians and economists can also bring about changes in the market.

The Movement of the Yen

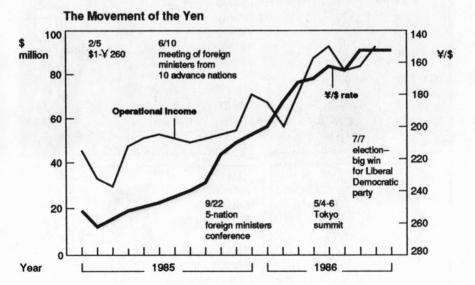

Because of the rise in the yen and the fall in crude oil prices, beginning in June 1986 nine electric companies and the leading gas company lowered their rates in order to return to consumers and manufacturers their marginal profit.

Ummm ... I haven't been to see her in a long time, but we talk a lot on the phone

That's fine

The reason I called you–I'm worried about Mitsutomo — especially since my home town is Imahama

Do you want to build the amusement park?

No ... Just now, the company is caught between a rock and a hard place

Personally, I'm against it

What? You know about that?

From a long-term perspective, I think we should be looking for new ways to attract business

Because Hitachi Manufacturing Company's exports are worth about $5 billion a year, if the yen rises one yen per dollar, the marginal loss is ¥5 billion. With a rise of one yen per dollar, Fujitsu shows a yearly loss of ¥1 billion.

SHIKOKU — IMAHAMA

Because of the rise in the yen, Hitachi expected 40% less profit in 1986 than in 1985. Therefore, from October 1986, it undertook the first cut in 11 years of workers' and management's pay.

The yen came into the world in 1871. At that time ¥1 equaled $1. In April 1949 the rate was set at ¥360 to $1.

The basis for setting the rate at ¥360 to $1 is not known. It is said that the Occupation leaders set that rate because they heard that *yen* means "circle," and a circle has 360 degrees.

hahaha

I see. You're really just a sheep in wolf's clothing!

... But what did Shijima say?

To buy people from the U.S.

But I thought there was nothing to buy from the U.S. any more

...

Except ... U.S. technical capabilities are still terrific

In August 1971, 100 years after the yen came into the world, Japan said farewell to the era when ¥360 equaled $1 and moved to a fluctuating-market system. The yen temporarily floated during the period of the "Nixon Shock."

Oh! Yuri!

Your friend Yuri is doing research at Princeton's Biotech Laboratory

Why not come to the U.S. with me and see her?

I'd like to, but I wonder if I can get off work ...

You can

Huh?

?

HA HA HA

Well! So it seems like you can do it!

Yes ... and afterward I'd like to arrange visits with a number of companies

From December 19, 1971, to February 14, 1973, the hard currency rate was known as the Smithsonian rate. This was a provisional fixed rate following the Nixon Shock.

At a 10-nation conference held at the Smithsonian Institution in Washington, the exchange rate was cut from ¥360 to ¥308 to the dollar. The yen's value increased 16.88%.

SEVERAL MONTHS LATER. IMAHAMA IS REBORN WITH THE COMING OF THE NEW HIGH-TECH CENTER

Thank you. It was all your doing

As a token of our gratitude ...

Much better, thank you

No no, I was just one person ...

Mr. Matsukawa, how are you feeling?

I am glad

Beginning in February 1973, countries moved one after another to the floating exchange-rate system. Basically, this marked the opening of a fluctuating market system. In October 1973, the oil crisis began, and the yen was hurled into a spiral of agitation.

3

Industrial Structure

There is much more to be gained by Manufacture than by Husbandry; and by Merchandise than Manufacture. But Holland and Zealand being seated at the mouths of three long great rivers passing through rich countries, do keep all the inhabitants upon the sides of those rivers but as husbandmen; whilst they themselves are the manufactors of their commodities: and do dispense them into all parts of the world, making returns for the same, at what prices almost they please themselves.

William Petty, *Political Arithmetic* (1690)

IN WHICH we see how changes in the international political climate have transformed Japan's industrial structure:

a delegation from Middle Eastern Country P seeks the resurrection of a Japanese-Middle East oil chemistry project and revives memories of the oil crisis of 1973;

the earlier adventures of Mitsutomo's Toda in the Middle East are recounted, as he sought a special pipeline to his company and discovered his own achilles heel;

the veteran businessman Akiyama reveals the shape of the new Japanese industrial structure, which has done away with the need for Country P's oil;

and executives at Mitsutomo discuss their company's relations with Country P with Kudo worrying about the long-term effects of a break and Tsugawa trying to cut losses.

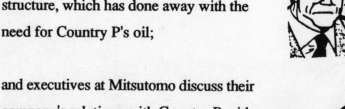

NARITA AIRPORT

They're here

The minister and vice-minister of industry from Country P have arrived!

THE MINISTER OF INDUSTRY FROM COUNTRY P

Japan's rate of economic growth greatly declined after the oil crisis. Before the crisis, it was 10%; after the first crisis, it fell to 5%, and to 3% after the second. Japan entered a period of low growth.

In 1880, primary industries made up 67.1% of manufacturing; in 1980, they had fallen to 3.6%; tertiary industries, which had been 23.9%, rose to 58.8%.

I have just passed around a summary of the demands Country P put forth at today's minister-level meeting

It contains specific requests for the return of the former king's Japanese property and for a loan, but

the main thrust, as you surmised, is the continuation of the oil chemistry project

How did they phrase that?

They said ...

"persist in putting the contract into effect"

As personal income increases, the weight of the labor force moves from primary to secondary and tertiary industries. This is called the Petty-Clark principle. It was discovered by Colin Clark.

ROTTERDAM, THE FOCUS OF SPOT OIL TRANSACTIONS

FROM THE MITSUTOMO OFFICE CAN BE SEEN A FOREST OF OIL TANKERS

THE MITSUTOMO ROTTERDAM OFFICE

What? There was a stock split?!

Really? Where?

At North Sea Brent

Stocks that were worth over $30 are now at $10 ... And there are rumors that the Saudis are increasing production ...

Shall I telex Tokyo?

The American economist Raymond Vernon's "product cycle theory" argues that the development of industry and its relation to trade are divided into three stages. Japan has already entered the third stage.

In 1966, the value of Japan's electronics projects was less than ¥1 trillion. By 1976, it had grown to ¥5 trillion; in 1981, it topped ¥10 trillion. Electronics became the second great industry, after automobiles.

129

THE WINDS OF THE OIL CRISIS WERE BLOWING THROUGHOUT JAPAN

WINTER 1973

THE PRIME MINISTER'S RESIDENCE

Mr. Foreign Minister, how is the Middle Eastern war going?

THE PRIME MINISTER IN 1973, TATAKA KAKUEI

The Middle Eastern war is easing into its middle phase, but because of the attitude of the Arab countries, oil is being held hostage

Has the oil really stopped coming?

Reports from the Middle East say that shipping is being delayed, but the amount already shipped is as usual

The real effects will be felt in the future

MINISTER OF MITI NAKANE

How much do you think the cut will be?

At the worst—30%

30%!?

In the second oil crisis, materials industries like aluminum refining, oil chemistry, and open–hearth furnaces received fatal wounds. They slumped, becoming structurally depressed industries because of rising costs, declining domestic demand, and a loss of international competitive power.

The coal industry experienced the cruelest form of change in industrial structure. Even the postwar leaders had to retrench completely because of increases in imported coal and changes to energy produced by oil.

THE MIDDLE EAST —
COUNTRY P

From 1949 to 1983, there were 1,876 companies listed on the Tokyo Stock
Exchange. Of these, 485 lost their places—1 out of 4 disappeared.

According to a survey conducted by *Nikkei Business*, the lifespan of an ordinary company is no more than 30 years. There seems to be a cycle of growth and decline for each company.

In the past, a necessary condition for the location of industry was proximity to a harbor. For most recent electronics industries, an airport is necessary, so that Oita, Miyazaki, and Kumamoto provide locations for industry.

FIVE YEARS LATER—NEAR THE BORDER BETWEEN COUNTRY P AND COUNTRY A

In the past, when heavy chemicals were a leading industry, "new industrial cities" were the focus of development. The nucleus of today's ultramodern industries is the "technopolis," which is expected to be the trump card of regional economic activation.

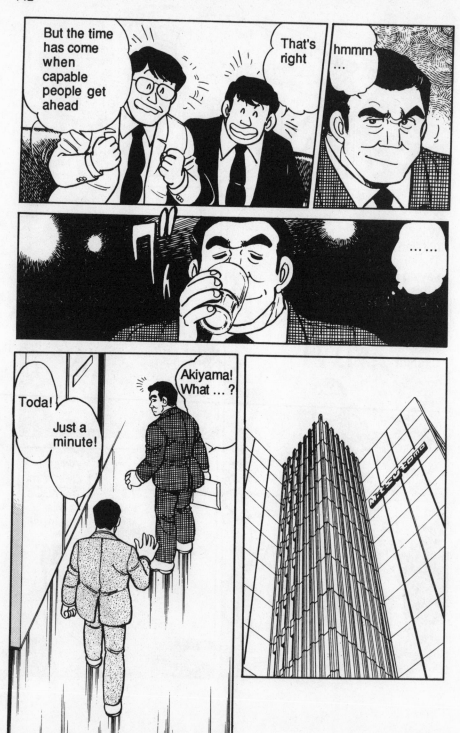

The relative increase in importance of a country's tertiary industries, and especially its service industries, is called "servicing" the economy. And an increase in the value of knowledge and services is called "softening."

Our information networks are highly sensitive!

Toda ...

Yes ...

As a precaution, watch out for religious connections

Hmph! That ...

... ...

It's not possible!

BUT — A FEW MONTHS LATER IN COUNTRY P

Daniel Bell suggests that when over 50% of all employees are in service industries, the economy is entering a period of softening and servicing. Right after the oil crisis, Japan entered this stage.

The measure of investment in information or services in order to manufacture things is called the "softening rate." From 1970 to 1980, the softening rate was increasing in most industries.

TOKYO—KASUMIGASEKI

OFFICES OF MINISTER NAKANE'S FACTION

In order for declining industries to remain alive, they need to advance into fields of growth outside their original industry. If over 3/4 of the sales of the leading shipbuilder are of products outside that industry, is the company a shipbuilder in name only?

Industries that left their original field and made remarkable advances are electronics, new materials, and biotechnology. Because the original company name often no longer fits, such industries are likely to change their names.

The aluminum refining industry received the most drastic effects of the oil crisis. Because the cost of electric power rose, the industry lost its competitive power, and its production of 1,650,000 tons shrank to 350,000 tons.

Once called the "rice of industry," iron and steel were Japan's great industrial mainstay. Because of a decrease in international competitive power and because of sluggish domestic demand, there was an "iron freeze" leaving the production of crude steel at less than 100 million tons.

During the 100 years up to 1980, U.S. primary industries fell from 50% to 4%, and secondary industries rose from 25% to 27%; tertiary industries increased sharply, from 25% to 69%.

Businesses related to raw materials were eclipsed

On the other hand, high-tech electronics and service industries had an astonishing success

There are people who say it trivialized the Japanese economy

or that it "softened" and "serviced" the economy

A reverse oil crisis!

When the price of oil got too high, people began to develop new oil fields and a formerly unimaginable situation arose

Yes! In Country P, it accomplished what revolution and war could not——it sent the oil chemistry project into dire straits—but at the time no one foresaw it

You can't say that the government's policy was completely mistaken

Although the industrial structure had been changing slowly for decades, the unexpected oil crisis speeded up the historic revolution

mmhmm. Because oil is still an important commodity for Japan

And Toda wears the scars

In fact, afterward, he kept climbing the ladder of success

Yes, but that incident will always be his Achilles heel

Many people in the company felt his future was determined by the way he handled that problem

Of course! That's why the veins in his face turn purple

and he yells at us

World War II had great meaning for the heavy industrialization of the Japanese economy. Before the war, agricultural and maritime products made up 46.6% and industrial products 44.5%, but after the war, agricultural products were greatly reduced and industrial products reached 56.8%.

The Oil Crisis and Japanese Economics

The two oil crises greatly reduced Japanese economic growth and suddenly changed the Japanese constitution. There was a shift from "heavy" industries like iron and steel and oil chemistry to "light" industries like electronics and precision instruments.

At the same time, individual industries increased their rate of "softening" (the proportion of investment in products decreased and the proportion of investment in non-products increased). There was a general tendency for the economy to "soften".

We can call an industry where the softening rate is over 40% a "soft industry". In 1970, 26.5% of all industries were soft; in 1975, 39.4% were soft; in 1980, there was a leap to 45.6%.

In the era of softening, small and middle-sized businesses, which have previously been pressed by large-scale businesses, are able to expand their fields of activity; new areas develop, which focus on the pioneer fields of venture business.

Changes in the Japanese Economy

	Before the Oil Crisis	After the Oil Crisis
General Characteristic	"Mass" economy	"Quality" economy
Era	High-speed growth	Information
Goal	Mass production	Perfection of quality (services, softening)
Industrial structure		
Special characteristic	Heaviness	Lightness
Operating principle	Profit from size	Profit from diversity
Strongest industry	Iron and steel	Electronics
	Automobiles	Communications
	(prosperity for great enterprises)	Biotechnology (venture business)
Attitude toward trade	Emphasis on exports	Emphasis on imports
Finance		
Character of government	Large government	Small government
Objects of public investment	Roads, bridges (national base)	Urban development Improvement of residential quality
Tax system	Primarily direct	Primarily indirect
Sources of capital	Indirect financing	Direct financing
Interest system	Set interest	Variable interest
Economic system	Keynes	Monetarism Supply-side economics
International environment		
International feeling	Inward	Outward
Currency system	Fixed market system	Variable market system
Share of world's GNP	5%	10%
Economic sphere	Era of the West	Era of the Pacific

Japan's economy industrialized furiously in the late 1950s and early 1960s. During that period, there was a fourfold increase in the metal and chemical industries and a sevenfold increase in the manufacture of machinery. During the same period, heavy industry increased from 40% to 60%.

If we distinguish between household expenditures for goods and for services, in 1970 goods cost 73% and services 27%. In 1975, the relative importance of services had increased: goods cost 65.5% and services 34.5%.

With changes in the industrial structure, changes also appeared in the trade structure. On the one hand, textile exports retreated; on the other hand, heavy chemical-industry products, which formed 40% of exports in 1960, rose to 80% in 1975.

Are industries that do not manufacture goods more profitable than industries that do? According to closing accounts for a three-month period in 1986, production industries had a 23.7% reduction in profits; non-production industries recorded a 17.3% increase in profits.

The U.S. economist Walt Rostow distinguishes 5 stages of economic development. He calls the third stage "take-off." Japan entered the take-off period at the end of the 19th century.

4

Deficit Finance

The sovereign has only three duties to attend to; three
duties of great importance, indeed, but plain and intelligible to
common understandings: first, the duty of protecting the society
from the violence and invasion of other independent societies;
secondly, the duty of protecting, as far as possible, every member of
the society from the injustice or oppression of every other member
of it, or the duty of establishing an exact administration of justice;
and, thirdly, the duty of erecting and maintaining certain public
works and certain public institutions.

Adam Smith, *The Wealth of Nations*

IN WHICH we see that deficit financing
is sometimes deficit finagling and
discover that recipients of social welfare
do not always fare well:

the mother of Mitsutomo's young Ueda
provides an opportunity to experience
firsthand the tribulations of life in a senior
citizens' home;

Kudo and Tsugawa discover that the
government can furnish the money for
social welfare projects but only human
beings can create social welfare;

thoughts of welfare expenditures conjure
up tales of Japan's postwar departure
from balanced budgets and fears of the
chaotic depression years, when deficit
finance began;

and a mutual need to stimulate the
economy leads Japan and the U.S. to
create a new currency and embark on a
program of joint investment.

The amount of government bonds issued at the end of fiscal 1987 is expected to be about ¥151 trillion. That enormous sum is about 3 times annual expenditures. This is as if a businessman had outstanding debts 3 times his yearly expenditures.

Isn't it good that the government isn't squandering our money?

Stupid! That's why our relations with the government are going to hell in a handbasket

Exactly … that old geezer went too far

At any rate, it's a problem when our relations with the government don't go smoothly

Leave it to me! I'll show you that the Welfare Ministry project is still a good investment

Oh … the plan for the senior citizens' village!

I'd like to come up with a model for the aging society of the future

RRRR

Conference room. What? I see

176

When the time comes to redeem previously issued government bonds, sometimes there is no source of revenue to redeem them. In those cases, new government bonds are issued to convert the loans in order to get the money to redeem the first bonds.

In 1986 total general expenditures were about ¥54 trillion; total revenue was about ¥43 trillion. This is like a household income of ¥430,000 and expenditures of ¥540,000.

uh ...
Miss Amamiya,
we're going out
...

Take
your
time

hmm

ha ha

THE PRIME MINISTER'S RESIDENCE

Based on rough estimates of needs for 1987, the national bonds increased about 25% over the previous year, to a record ¥14 trillion. They made of 1/4 of the budget, and interest payments alone were over ¥10 trillion.

The Federal Reserve Board (FRB) can be considered the central U.S. bank. Twenty-three Federal Reserve banks join to form the central banking system, and its administrative organ is the FRB.

Just so the economy improves before the election, it will be OK

But if inflation weakens the dollar, it will make things tough for Japan and Europe

Well, Japan is carrying a big financial deficit

So Japan is hoping for inflation too?

Then let's get going on a "policy of international cooperation" ... he he he

JAPAN—KASUMIGASEKI

THE WELFARE MINISTRY

Incredible! The more the employees, the more the paperwork!

That's Parkinson's law!

SHH! Don't talk so loud!

Or we'll have to bring the same amount for each prefecture

Huh? 46 loads?

"As economies develop, public finances tend to expand." (German economist Adolph Wagner)

If the Izu Nagaoka senior citizens' village is approved, a similar one will be built in every prefecture

Well, that's fine

By the way, has your mom come to Tokyo?

um ... yeah

Of course!

That's why you can't go out at night!

Don't make fun of me! I've got real problems

It turns out that Mom came because she had a fight with my sister-in-law. She's really stubborn ...

Oh my!

186

In 1984, the cost of Japanese medical care was ¥15 trillion. Treating one person cost ¥125,500. The total was an increase of ¥550 billion from 1983 and of ¥10 trillion from 1973.

It has a recreation room, a reading room, a gymnasium, a lounge, a health center

The recreation room has a sing-along set

Well, it's certainly well planned

This figure exactly uses up the estimate

WELFARE MINISTRY OFFICIAL KOBAYASHI

I'll have my superior take a look at this plan

Thank you very much

The rate of increase in national health-care costs from 1983 to 1984 was 3.8%, less than the rate of increase in national income of 5.2%. From February 1984, there were wide repercussions from a new requirement that businessmen take responsibility for 10% of their health-care costs.

I'm being used to reconcile my mother with my sister-in-law

Well, well! Show me too

SUNSHINE HOME

MONTHLY FEE: ¥70,000

It sure costs a lot, doesn't it!

......

Yeah! It's like a high-class condo-minium

The price goes with the environment and the facilities, but ...

Even so, you can't pay the fee on your salary

In many cases, local self-governing bodies act as agents for national policies in fields such as public works, social security, and education. The government gives subsidies to the local areas; 70% of the combined regional and national tax revenues are used by the local areas.

Japan's population is rapidly aging. In 1985, 10.1% of the people were over 65; by the year 2000, the percentage is expected to increase to 15.6%.

Along with the aging of the population, the number of people who receive public pensions is increasing every year by over 1 million. At present, each person who receives a pension is supported by 9 people, but by the year 2010, each will be supported by 3.

The estimated cost of social services in 1986 was ¥4.2 trillion for the national treasury's share of health-care costs, ¥2.9 trillion for pensions, ¥2.7 trillion for welfare — a total of ¥9.8 trillion. This was 18.2% of the national budget.

When government bonds are issued in large amounts, money market and capital market funds are siphoned into the state; the supply and demand of capital becomes stringent; and it becomes difficult to supply capital to businesses and the public sector. This is called "crowding out."

The country can issue special government bonds that are limited to allotments for public enterprises. These construction bonds are like long-term home loans, because the public capital remains for future generations.

So, what about Ueda's mother?

The other day his brother and wife went to see her. She made them kiss her feet and then went home proud as a peacock!

hehehe! That's terrific!

Still ...

When you're spending as much as the national debt, and the burden falls on the people ... you'd like to make your money go as far as possible

Definitely ... was it in 1965

that they issued the first deficit bonds?

Yes. I'll never forget the recession of 1965.

One after another, big securities companies and corporations went bankrupt— and we were scurrying around too

Deficit government bonds are a source of revenue to pay operating expenses and personnel costs; government bonds are loans that remain for future generations. Therefore an increase in deficit bonds mean a loss in financial health.

I'm getting old too

That was over 20 years ago

THE PRIME MINISTER'S RESIDENCE

The 1965 recession?

That was the year we issued deficit bonds

Finance Ministers Tataka and Fukuba were really in a spot, weren't they?

……

MAY 28, 1965. IN THE BANK OF JAPAN

THAT EVENING. THE RIVERBANK OF JAPAN INN

...

It is unprecedented for the Bank of Japan to supply special financing for just one company

SASAKI DEN, VICE PRESIDENT OF THE BANK OF JAPAN

In 1965, 59.4% of tax revenues were from direct taxes. Every year the rate increased: in 1970 it was 66.3%; in 1985, it was 73.4%

In 1975, the national debt was ¥1 trillion. After that, it gradually increased: in 1985, when the large-scale redemption of government bonds issued after 1975 began, it amounted to ¥20 trillion.

Budget balancing requires expenditures to be within the limits of revenues. Its opposite is Keysian financial policy, which urges the use of constructive deficit financing in response to the business climate.

1931 — THE DEPRES-SION WAS PARTICU-LARLY BAD IN FARMING VILLAGES ... HIT HARD BY PLUMMETING RICE AND SILKWORM PRICES, THE UNEM-PLOYED FILLED THE CITIES.

IN FEBRUARY 1932 — ABOUT THE SAME TIME AS THE MAN-CHURIAN INCIDENT — FORMER PRIME MINISTER INOUE JUNNOSUKE WAS FELLED BY RIGHT-WING TERRORISTS. THEN PRIME MINISTER INUKAI WAS MURDERED DURING THE MAY 15 INCIDENT.

IN 1932 FINANCE MINISTER TAKAHASHI KOREKIYO SPOKE TO THE DIET.

We will practice positive finance by issuing government bonds guaranteed by the Bank of Japan

By the Bank of Japan?

The bank will print money and buy up the government's bonds

And the government will revive business with that money?

Then it will undertake public works projects in the villages

Of course! That way we can mobilize the industries that are idle because of the crisis

The increase in military expenditures will invigorate the munitions industry

Tax revenues will also increase

So, it's two birds — no, three! — with one stone

Look, Ma — no hands!

IN 1930, THE SITUATION BEGAN TO IMPROVE. TAKAHASHI MADE A SPEECH TO THE DIET: "NOW THAT PROSPERITY HAS RETURNED, THERE IS A DANGER OF INFLATION. I WILL DECREASE THE NATIONAL DEBT AND MILITARY EXPENDITURES."

In 1949, Joseph Dodge came to Japan from the U.S. in order to deal with Japanese inflation. He made drastic cuts in the financial system and enforced the Economic Stabilization Program, which insisted on a balanced budget. This is known as the "Dodge Line."

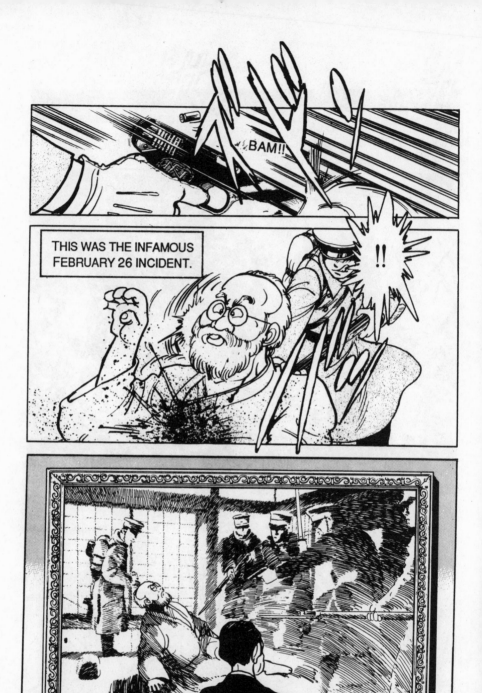

Monetarists charge that the Keynesians' stress on the role of the government leads to the creation of large inefficient governments and a loss in economic energy .

M2 is an index that expresses the supply of money; it refers to currency + liquid deposits + fixed-term deposits. Monetarists believe that changes in the money supply exert the greatest influence on the price of goods.

The Swelling of the National Debt

Ten years have passed since the cry of financial danger first was raised. What is financial danger? To put it simply, it is the disequilibrium that arises when the amount of money a country spends for public works, social security, and other services greatly exceeds the amount of money it takes in from taxes and other forms of revenue.

As the figure below shows, the General Accounting budget for expenditures was about ¥54 trillion. Income was about ¥41 trillion – a difference of about ¥13 trillion. This difference is provided by loans: in 1986, ¥11 trillion worth of government bonds were issued, or 20.2% of the government's income. This situation, where 20 to 30 percent of the government's income comes from loans, has continued for nearly 10 years. A household could not survive under these conditions.

What is the scale of these government bonds or loans? They have accumulated in great amounts since 1975: in June 1983, they topped ¥100 trillion; as of March 1987, they were worth ¥143 trillion. This is as if each person in Japan had loaned the government ¥1.2 million.

A loan earns interest, and when its term is up it must be repaid. Nor can the operating expenses of a loan be taken lightly. The operating costs of paying the interest on government bonds in 1981 was ¥6.7 trillion (the interest itself was ¥5.6 trillion); according to the budget for 1985, it surpassed ¥10 trillion, replacing the cost of social security as the greatest expense.

In 1985, the government began to redeem the great number of bonds issued in the previous 10 years. It had to issue conversion bonds to pay for the redemption; these were estimated in 1986 at ¥11.5 trillion. It is a dangerous situation when a government has to borrow money to pay off its loans.

Income–1986
(in ¥ trillion; % in parentheses)

Expenditures–1986
(in ¥ trillion; % in parentheses)

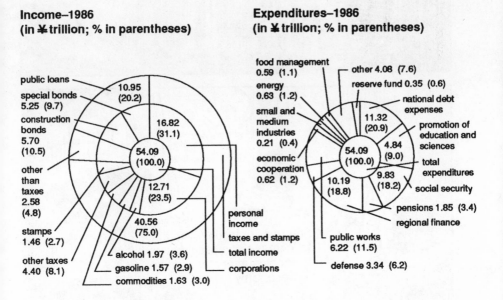

Income–1986:
public loans
special bonds 5.25 (9.7)
construction bonds 5.70 (10.5)
other than taxes 2.58 (4.8)
stamps 1.46 (2.7)
other taxes 4.40 (8.1)
10.95 (20.2)
16.82 (31.1)
54.09 (100.0)
12.71 (23.5)
40.56 (75.0)
alcohol 1.97 (3.6)
gasoline 1.57 (2.9)
commodities 1.63 (3.0)
personal income
taxes and stamps
total income
corporations

Expenditures–1986:
food management 0.59 (1.1)
energy 0.63 (1.2)
small and medium industries 0.21 (0.4)
economic cooperation 0.62 (1.2)
other 4.08 (7.6)
reserve fund 0.35 (0.6)
national debt expenses
promotion of education and sciences
total expenditures
social security
pensions 1.85 (3.4)
regional finance
public works 6.22 (11.5)
defense 3.34 (6.2)
11.32 (20.9)
54.09 (100.0)
4.84 (9.0)
9.83 (18.2)
10.19 (18.8)

The people who pay indirect taxes are not the people who actually bear the burden for them. Taxes on liquor, gas and oil, commodities, transit, admissions, automobile weight, and playing cards are all indirect taxes.

According to the National Tax Administration Agency, 90.9% of all Japanese businessmen pay taxes (1983). If we exclude persons in the lowest bracket, all businessmen pay taxes.

90% of all businessmen pay taxes; only 39.5% of all self-employed people pay, and only 14.6% of all farmers. This is popularly known as 9-4-1 (*ku-shi-pin*).

Taxes are withheld from 100% of a businessman's income, from only 50% of the income of a self-employed person filing his own return, and from only 30% of a farmer's income. This is known as 10-5-3 (*to-go-san*).

5

A Monetary Revolution

At 6 percent compound interest, money doubles in value every 12 years. It has been estimated that the $24 received by the Indians for Manhattan Island would, if deposited at compound interest, be today worth as much as all real property on the island. At 6 percent, Sir Francis Drake's plunder of Spanish gold would today equal Britain's wealth.

Paul A. Samuelson, *Economics*

IN WHICH we see how the monetary revolution of the 1970s and 1980s has stimulated corporate speculative financing, sometimes with disastrous consequences:

a body floating in the Thames spawns worries at Mitsutomo, sending Tsugawa abroad to investigate and revisit scenes of past dalliances;

a tottering Mitsutomo fi-tech scheme reveals the close connections of both the Vatican and the Mafia with the world of international finance;

an old friend of Kudo's explains the mysteries of banking and securities and opens important doors for him;

and Kudo arranges a transaction that turns the collapse of a Milan bank into an advantage for Mitsutomo and saves Tsugawa's hide in the process.

LONDON

BESIDE THE THAMES

There are two types of interest on deposits: a fixed rate, as in bank deposits, and a rate that goes up and down according to market fluctuations. Recently there has been an increase in the picking and choosing of interest and a number of high-interest fluctuating types have appeared.

TODAY THE
BODY OF A MAN
WAS FOUND
FLOATING IN THE
VICINITY OF
BLACKFRIARS
BRIDGE, NEAR
THE LONDON
FINANCIAL
DISTRICT KNOWN
AS THE CITY.

HE WAS ABOUT 60 YEARS OLD.

JUDGING FROM THE QUALITY OF HIS SUIT, HE WAS A MAN OF WEALTH.

HOWEVER, THE POLICE HAVE NOT BEEN ABLE TO DISCOVER A CLUE TO HIS IDENTITY.

Japan's financial revolution was triggered by 3 K's: *kokusai* (national debt), *kokusaika* (internationalization), and *kikaika* (mechanization). The issuing of a large national bond stimulated the development of public bond markets, and with internationalization and mechanization it became possible to do business quickly over a wide area.

JAPAN —
SEVERAL
DAYS LATER

WHO WAS
THE MAN IN
THE
THAMES?

WAS THE
MYSTERY
MAN
ENRIQUE,
PRESIDENT
OF BANCO
DA VINCI?

The
whereabouts
of Banco da
Vinci
president
Enrique are
unknown …

Enrique disappeared from his home in Milan about 10 days ago

......

It looks like he won't be able to get in touch with us

The paper doesn't say whether it was suicide or murder

I think he was killed!

uh huh

Was Enrique likely to burn his bridges behind him?

No ... his bank was the foremost in Italy, and he was a member of Milan's financial world ... only —

The first step to financial liberalization is the lowering of barriers between banks and securities. If banks begin to buy and sell previously issued bonds, they can begin to develop joint offshoots such as the Chugoku Fund, a "securities company for ordinary savings."

Only what ...?!

There was a rumor that he was involved in a struggle within the Vatican

So I heard

If it's the Vatican, it's awkward

Anyway, it's your baby... Straighten it out

It'll be a major problem if a plan like this falls through

I want you to fly to London and Milan to check things out personally

Yes

In Japan, the operations of banks and securities companies are criss-crossed by the 65 provisions of the Securities Trading Law. The main purpose of this law is to protect depositors, but recently, with liberalization, its significance has changed.

SEVERAL MONTHS BEFORE — IN MILAN

I apologize for using my rooms to discuss business with you, but ...

The Japanese-American Yen-Dollar Committee was created when President Reagan visited Japan. Decisions made by it had great significance for Japan's internationalization.

Borrowing by banks from depositors is called indirect financing; the borrowing of capital by issuing stocks or securities is called direct financing.

Signor Tsugawa, has our chief bond dealer explained to you our bank's situation?

Yes ... Everything seems right in line. I'll consult with Tokyo, and I should have a decision in a day or two

BANCO DA VINCI

Generally, even among institutions described as banks, there are a number of different operations; there can be ordinary banks, long-term credit banks, trust banks, foreign exchange banks, mutual finance banks, credit unions, and credit associations.

ENGLAND

MITSUTOMO TRADING COMPANY'S LONDON OFFICE

Among ordinary banks, there are metropolitan banks, with their headquarters in major cities, and regional banks, with their headquarters in regional centers. In Japan, there are 13 metropolitan banks. They have less than 20% of the capital of all financial institutions.

Oh! Mr. Tsugawa

The man's identity has been confirmed. It is definitely Enrique

Tentatively, the cause of death is suicide

Has something come to light?

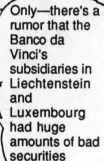

Suicide?

They are feverishly gathering information in the City, but they haven't announced anything concrete yet

Only—there's a rumor that the Banco da Vinci's subsidiaries in Liechtenstein and Luxembourg had huge amounts of bad securities

There is also a story that money was flowing to the Mafia

Can they get a sense of da Vinci's situation?

There's a business report, but...in addition to the actual da Vinci firm, there are holding companies and foreign local corporations and paper companies to avoid taxes

Since there is a spiderweb of subsidiary companies, we can't grasp the actual situation

If the authorities in the City move together to recover the debts, won't da Vinci go under?

The bankers here all think that if they do, it won't be able to avoid default

mmm... do you think so?

I don't know for sure, but if even one of the rumors turns out to be true, it's a big possibility

Didn't da Vinci have backers?

Oh... you're thinking of the Vatican?

It used a variety of disguises, but the fact is that the Vatican was one of the major shareholders in the bank

There is no big difference between the operations of a regional bank and a metropolitan bank, but the total capital of all 63 regional banks is about 1/2 the capital of the 13 metropolitan banks. They have many operations intimately connected to their regions, such as the handling of the capital of regional self-governing bodies.

GYUGG

So ... your plan came out to withdraw the Vatican's capital and devise a "fi-tech" scheme. You really tripped up

I-I have no excuse

Now opposition is growing in our company to earning money by investments ... That hurts more than the amount we lost

Enterprises do not merely collect the capital their main companies need; they also use the capital on hand profitably. This use of the profit margin is called "fi-tech," or speculative financing. Recently, fi-tech has been encouraged by an expansion of possible methods.

A long-term credit bank is constructed in accord with the Long-Term Credit Bank Law. At present there are 3 such banks: the Long-Term Credit Bank of Japan, the Industrial Bank of Japan, and the Debenture and Credit Bank of Japan. Their primary business is long-term capital loans.

Steps in the Financial Revolution

In the U. S., the birthplace of the financial revolution, inflation called forth a period when depositors picked their interest rates carefully; it brought about financial changes that centered on the liberalization of interest and the mutual advance of currency and securities.

In Japan the financial revolution was triggered by the issuance of large amounts of government bonds. In direct response to the first oil crisis, in 1973, the Japanese economy fell into an unprecedented slump. In order to overcome it, the government instituted large-scale public investment, but because the recession had created a shortage of funds, the issuance of large amounts of government bonds was inevitable.

Changes in Public Bonds

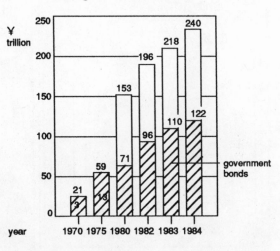

¥ trillion

government bonds

year   1970 1975 1980 1982 1983 1984

In the circulating bond market, public corporations multiplied rapidly. At the same time, the interest system — which had been artificially constructed up to that point — changed markedly, and new, high-interest methods of saving appeared.

The U. S. financial revolution abolished a number of restraints; Japan also moved toward liberalization as it lowered the barrier between banking and securities companies.

There is another important element in Japan's financial revolution: financial internationalization. As trade friction continued, currency friction became a sore point between the U. S. and Japan, and measures were adopted to ease restrictions on foreign banks and to liberalize exchange transactions.

The types of financial resources suddenly multiplied; businesses were invigorated as they began to profit from the international financial markets.

As financial liberalization gathered momentum, it awakened previously dormant areas. New services appeared, such as "electro-banking", which is linked to computers and communications technology. No one knows where this revolution will end.

Japan's Financial Liberalization

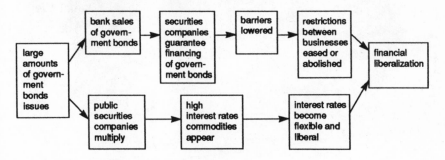

250

The primary business of a trust bank is to amass capital by loan trusts or cash trusts and to make long-term loans to businesses. Recently, the areas of activity have multiplied to include pension trusts and land trusts.

Even so, it's an impossible situation.

The European financial world is in chaos. Then besides, a murder by the Mafia or someone ... there are unimaginable rumors about the business community

That Tsugawa got himself hooked up with quite a scoundrel in Enrique

The international financial world is certainly a rogues' gallery ...

For years, there have been stories of swindles

It's not a field that amateurs dabble in lightly

But Mr. Akiyama, aren't we entering the era of finance?

Companies like M Automobiles are revising their articles of corporation so they can make a profit not just from making and selling cars but from finance

Mutual finance banks, based on the Mutual Finance Bank Law, are financial institutions aimed at the small and middle firms of stock company organizations. In addition to performing the usual business of banks, they are unique in acting as mutual aid societies, since they developed from mutual loan companies. At present, there are 69 in Japan.

Credit unions are small to medium-sized special financial organizations; they are non-profit membership groups. In principle, loans are made to members. Credit associations have a similar organization; their members are local small businessmen and workers.

In the U.S., banking and securities are separated under the Glass-Steagall Act. This law arose from the lessons of the Great Depression. It was intended to prevent excessive competition for savings and to protect depositors.

Do they intend to enter stock-broking in earnest?

They seem to

In the U.S., financial methods are multiplying and the field of activity is growing

Mitsutomo is studying it too, but no matter what, there's a shortage of talent

What if they came here?

Don't be stupid

Since Mitsutomo wants to do it, I'd encourage them to go to Europe

Europe?

In addition to Eurodollar business, there will soon be an increase in Euroyen transactions

Do you know the word Jal-pak?

No ...

Recently, Japanese businesses offered bonds for sale in Europe

They collected a lot of money on profitable terms

The yen that moves in the far-off European money markets of London and Zurich is called the Euroyen. Deposits of Euroyen (including those in Asia) are said to equal ¥10 trillion (1985).

Once the financial revolution arrives, a number of regulations will probably be removed

Japan and the U.S. will have to become like Europe

That's why it would be good to study in Europe ... We shouldn't miss a chance like this Jal-pak

But even so, we'll be starting from zero

Why?

If Mitsutomo is serious, I'll lend them my strength. "The cobbler knows his last."
All sorts of information come into my office

Of course ... Jal-pak

Even the Japanese financial institutions with the weakest administrative foundation are managed so that their operations will be effective. Using the "convoy system," they single out the most efficient operators and follow them.

Although his remains were returned to Italy, it seems that there has been a delay

Tomorrow they are finally going to conduct a funeral

Even so, why go to the funeral of someone like him?

Well ...

He put one over on you. I want to pay my respects

... the light of truth shines on all men ... he came into the world ... he was part of the world ... yet the world did not know him ...

A CEMETERY IN THE SUBURBS OF MILAN

The trend toward mobilizing credit in small securities is called "securitization." Mortgage certificates are one example. When there is a change from loans to raising money by securities, the flow of money also changes.

The essential elements of banking are changing greatly. Banks are using computers and communications circuits freely; electronic banking is developing and offering new services as the mechanization of bank operations progresses.

Among other things, the financial revolution of London's "City" liberalized the commissions of securities companies. It has been called the "big bang" because it seemed like a universal explosion. It was a great revolution that bet on the survival of the City's financial transactions.

Financial futures refer to the selling of financial commodities such as securities, cash, or stock indexes by the same methods that are used in commodities transactions involving red beans, rubber, or soybeans.

269

But the claims on da Vinci will continue as part of the investment? hmmm!

The Gottfert Bank was the bank least damaged in the recent affair

And because the Swiss managers have been conducting a sound enterprise, the people in management are all good

Our banks are always looking toward Europe, where "universal banking" is possible

When our company succeeds in buying Gottfert, it will shock the financial world!

The most valuable part of this purchase is Gottfert's talented people, since they've been trained in the sharpshooting financial world of Zurich

We have to be careful not to injure their pride in this transaction

In Japan and the U.S., the joint operation of banks and securities companies is prohibited in principle, but in Europe, it is even possible to combine trust and securities operations. This is called "universal banking."

But … you heard what the Vatican said, didn't you?

"Although the Gottfert makes a good profit …"

The Vatican probably needed a lot of money to settle the da Vinci affair

Anyway, since we're talking about a debt of millions of dollars

that should spur on our company's fi-tech program

…

The Third Bank On-Line System aims to link up networks not only of CDs and ATMs but of homes and businesses, allowing people to receive banking services without leaving home. And so we move toward the count-down.

I'm home

Is she asleep?

……?

?

Oh! You're home!

I'm sorry, I didn't realize it

What are you calculating so seriously? It doesn't look like the household accounts

This? Which pays more—the new government fund or discount bonds?

Oh?

I wonder what the official rate will be

Official rate? I never thought I'd hear those words coming from your lips!

Well, it's common among housewives! Many of us have made money in stocks

According to the statistics it's common for us to invest part of our annual income

So we are concerned about the direction of the official rate even more than the direction of our husband's salary

Government bonds are the illegitimate children of deficit financing, but government savings bonds are popular. The first to appear were middle-term government bond funds, followed by fixed-term government bond trust accounts and government discount bond accounts.

6

Epilogue

The changes that we see here as portents make themselves felt in
organizations composed of rather soft, small-scale units. They
mark the arrival not of abstractly organized systems but of
companies in which every individual in a human relationship is
given serious consideration. In the future, when more
people return to these soft groups and begin to live while
actually seeing their neighbors, for the first time we will live in
a society that is clearly different from societies of the industrial
age. The reason is that during the three hundred years of the
industrial age, we had a hard, combative production system; the
countryside was made up of a vague mass society in which
people's faces were not visible; the human groups that should
have been in between were only rarely known.

Yamazaki Shōwa, *The Birth of Soft Individualism*

IN WHICH we get a glimpse of the Japanese economy of the future and ponder some of the weighty decisions that it will require:

Mitsutomo's impending development of service industries cooks up dreams of pate for Tsugawa and tomatoes for Kudo;

Tsugawa and Kudo bump into hard truths about themselves as they realize that the business world needs the talents of both of them;

Kudo explains the workings of the economic god's unseen hand with some down-to-earth talk about pencils;

and the young Ueda discovers his vocation and vows to venture forth bringing human feelings to the logic of economics.

Food producers, which have custody of the nation's stomach, are the next great industry after electrical appliances and vehicle parts in the amount of shipping they do. In 1984, this was worth ¥2.57 trillion, 10.8% of the total for all manufacturing industries.

The giants of food production have special characteristics. Their small-scale operations are dispersed throughout the country so that their local ties are close and strong, and there are many varieties of businesses.

I'd like to go to Dreamrise Village in Mie Prefecture …

The Equal Employment Opportunity Law went into effect in April 1986. It prohibits discrimination in retirement or dismissals, making it the obligation of businesses to work toward the end of discrimination in recruiting, employment, placement, and promotions.

It is said that Japanese work too hard. The hours worked each year are less in Japan than in Korea or Thailand, but they exceed those of the Western developed nations by 200-500.

It was fine when we were in West Germany

That was the happiest time of our marriage

But after we came back, he changed

and then, I too

No ... it's just that his responsibilities became heavy

You know what that place is like

I understand how busy it gets

but I wish he'd think a little about me and the children

......

Recently the children have begun to realize that we don't get along

Well, I shouldn't talk. I'm not such a good husband, but, husbands and wives need to talk, to try to understand the other person instead of only asserting their own needs ...

That's easier said than done

When the per capita GNP is over $10,000, a country's economic activity suddenly declines and its growth rate decreases. This is called the "$10,000 trap"; it has been a common experience in the U.S. and the countries of Europe.

I owe you an apology

I must have seemed like an ass

Why? It's not important. It's more important to try to understand how Reiko feels

...

It may be trite, but you and I are economic animals

Because of us, the Japanese economy is on the rise and Japan is becoming an economic giant

but what about the cultural side ... at home, things haven't changed

In 1981, Japan's per capita GNP passed $10,000. In 1950, the year Japan extricated itself from its postwar period of chaos, the per capita GNP was $300; in 1965, it was $1,000; in 1976, it was $5,000.

In 1985, Japan's GNP passed ¥300 trillion. Japan boasts of a GNP that is 3d in the world, after only the U.S. and the USSR. These economic superpowers hold about 10% of the entire world's GNP.

If we try to predict the economics of the year 2010—Japan's per capita GNP will have joined the U.S.'s at the highest level in the world; Europe will continue its long-term decline; Korea and Taiwan will be making great leaps forward.

DREAMRISE VILLAGE,
MIE PREFECTURE

In Japan, government, business, and workers preserve a cooperative relationship, not the confrontational relationship found in Europe. This is called the "Japanese mix"; it is a driving force of Japan's economic development.

The clincher is that we don't use organic fertilizer or herbicides but raise them as naturally as possible

Hello!

Oh, yes

Mr. Kudo, this is Mr. Nakagawa of the Ministry of Agriculture and Forestry and Mr. Nagasaki of Keidanren

How do you do?

We're absolutely bowled over by Nagata's techniques

hahaha

I'd like to share these with city people who have to eat expensive tasteless food

Farmers shouldn't be called subsidy leeches — they've got what it takes!

According to the Ministry of Agriculture and Forestry, the price of the rice of Japanese producers is 7.5 times the international price; that of wheat is 5.9 times the international price; sugar 3.4 times; beef 3.1 times; pork 1.4 times. This is because of the government's policy of artificial protection.

According to a white paper on Japanese lifestyles issued on October 24, 1986, Japan is becoming the most affluent country in the world. Hereafter, it should carve out "previously untrodden roads to new affluence."

According to the white paper, service expenditures connected with house rent, land rent, clothing, and health-care insurance are falling; restaurant, transportation, and communications service expenses are rising.

In *Wealth of Nations*, Adam Smith says that economic self-interest led by the unseen hand of God enriches the world.

To make pencils, we use the absolutely straight cedars of

northern California or Oregon

We need many tools—chain-saws and ropes and trucks to bring the felled trees to the railroad siding

To make the saws and the engines, we must mine for minerals and make crude steel

then refine

9

and temper it

And for the logging, we must boil water for tea or coffee

and build cabins and dining halls and beds and showers

W. Stanley Jevons has suggested that the climate—and therefore the market—is closely related to the growth of sunspots. This theory has recently been revised; it now agrees with the 50-year-wave theory of Nikolai Kondratieff.

It's not that someone somewhere gives an order

Pencils are made right before our eyes, but it seems like a miracle

And everything sends out signals of value

That's why I believe in the god of economics

Mr. Kudo explained the logic of the economy well...

but farming and medicine and education probably shouldn't progress according to logic

When you force medicine or education into the logic of economics, it's rather unpleasant

But when farming loses to the logic of economics, doesn't industry get stronger?

The previously mentioned report of April 1986 defined Japan's long-term economic needs: (1) a residential policy that focuses on increased domestic consumption; (2) a financial policy that focuses on mechanized operations; (3) a revision of the Maruyama System, which does not tax interest on savings; (4) an increase in the importation of agricultural products.

In 1985, the number of Japanese traveling overseas was about 5 million; the number of Japanese living abroad also increased sharply. On the other hand, the number of foreigners employed in Japan and the number of foreign students is small. It seems that, compared to goods, the internationalization of people is slow.

The future of the Japanese economy is great; it is unusually bright
...

HERMAN KAHN HAS SAID THAT BECAUSE PEOPLE—ESPECIALLY JAPANESE—DO NOT LIVE BY BREAD ALONE, JAPAN MUST MAKE MANY CHOICES

The role of commerce in Japan's economy is great. In 1984, the transactions of the leading 9 companies made up 31% of the GNP, 44% of all export duties, 61% of all imports. Its role in international society is also great.

EACH OF THESE CHOICES WILL HAVE GREAT MEANING FOR THE WORLD OF THE FUTURE.

HEREAFTER, THEY WILL BE CONSIGNED TO HISTORY AS EVENTS OF SIGNIFICANCE.